SILENT WORDS THAT WERE NEVER SAID

Don A. Harris

To order additional copies of this book, contact:
Xlibris Corporation
1-888-795-4274
www.Xlibris.com
Orders@Xlibris.com
35057

CONTENTS

CHAPTER ONE

CHAPTER TWO

CHAPTER THREE

CHAPTER FOUR

CHAPTER ONE

The Last Lonely Day

Again, the bitter taste of loneliness destroys
the continuity of my mental palate.
Friendship, a longtime adversary
bathes in the pool of despair,
as my smiles of hope feed my hunger
for companionship.

My arms, exhausted from extending,
for one embracement of life
gives suicide a strong hold over my true desires.
Self-worth, my anchor to the ship of survival,
drags on the bottom of my soul searching for
the reef of belief and goodwill, only to grab
hold after the gunshots of failure free my soul
as anger and hatred flows down my face
from the hole of disbelief in my head
that soon makes a red pool of death that
marks the doorway to the end.

War Of The Worlds

Two lonely spots of light peer at each other from millions of miles away.
Neither of them aware of the light in the distance was planning to make war.
Not the war mankind had perfected like a meal from a world-class chef,
But the kind that erodes the soul like acid on a wedding cake.
Complete utter destruction with a splash of chocolate filling.

I, too, did not see the signs. They look like us. They even use our language.
Only if I could have looked into her soul, I would have clearly seen her plan
to destroy me.
By using my loyalty to cover up the coming of the end, I ran to the town folk
but they laughed and said "Women are our friends.

Now completely alone I hide.
My world gone, aliens all about.
But seconds before I lose my mind and succumb to the shame of failure,
she looked at me at that moment with a smile.
I throw myself in the fire and I scream, "You can have the world, but not
my soul!"

The Mistress

Loving and cunning is the cat that wants no home.
Feline mischief makes a relationship out of nothing,
but she cries for devotion, whines about commitment,
but only the commitment to her.

She builds a nest for a king, but hopes to trap a fool,
for in the land of lies, this is the only tool.
I warn you of tomorrow because this is my life today.
Leave a cup of milk on the porch and tell her to go away.

Haunted Minds

Picture a house filled with the dreams of how people view you.
As you enter through the door, black cats screech of your oncoming fate.
The living room has a party celebrating your demise
as you sit in the midst of their happiness,
your wrongdoings flash before your eyes.
Now you remember, you killed all of these people
and this is your hell.

As you walk upstairs, the first door opens and the two kids
you strangled appear—now the rope is around your neck.
You feel it tighten, and slowly you die.
Suddenly your eyes open, and a hand is holding your head under water
and the old lady you drowned is taking your life.

You run down the hall and a knife goes through your heart
and the storekeeper smiles his revenge.
You see bright lights and you think your hell is over.
Suddenly it comes clear, the gas enters the chamber
and reality comes for you.
It's your turn on Death Row.

Inner Turmoil

You open the pit of fear and realize
the depths of a wasteful life

Weakness flows through your veins and
the thoughts of others govern your state of mind.

Goodwill is only administered when profit
smiles greedily up from hell and every
dream is you falling deeper into the beliefs
of others.

The thought of communicating cuts your tongue
out and burns it in a pool of lies.

Truth's strong hand chokes you until the
very essence of fear leaves from your lungs
and with your first breath, fear will always
be your friend and truth your mentor.

Dark Dream

Dark skies send me running from fear
Corridors of fire guide me closer
to my hidden hell.

Pictures of friends melt on the walls
The smell of their burning flesh installs
the reality of the end. And as I
open the door to freedom,
the vacuum of time pulls me down
to the sharp spikes of despair.

As I lay riddled with holes,
my only escape is to free my soul
by leaving my body on the drops of my blood.
As my heart stops, my spirit leaps into the clouds.

I open my eyes and have to relive my fears,
only now as reality.

Is This Me?

An empty room is filled with my pain
but as you enter, it dissipates into
the foul smell of loneliness.

Each corner is another turning point
against my battle with fear.

Bravery is only represented by my inability
to kill myself while there is still time.
Day and night are the same in this room
because neither brings home comfort.

The lack of air in the room illustrates
that life is dead with fear.
My need to breathe is only a trick
by the room to make me reveal my
last drops of pain.
The lifeblood of an empty room.

Look At The Eyes

Peering out at the courtyard, time has no meaning.
Days turn into nights and the eyes come every hour.
Cold, different but always the same.
I wonder if the eyes have souls?
They only speak with their silences
and yet the eyes fear contact with the mind.
Loneliness smells like rotting fish in an alley
But this is the only sense left to me.
Look at the eyes, life in prison will always look the same.

Rescue My Soul

As I sit and free fall through time,
the small things in life grow into the
wall that keeps me from happiness.

Often pride supersedes wisdom in my plight
for truth and I still fall further from
contact with others.

Love with its many faces is
always a stranger in my heart.
The calling for help dies quickly in
disbelief and I fall deeper in mental collapse.

Shadows appear without light
and death calms my nerves
for in silence, life is reborn
and the graveyard of past sins
is now my crib of life.

Afraid To See

A parking lot of blind drivers fill all the spaces in your mind
The doors are locked with fear and humanity has thrown away the key
Even though we have so far to go.

History is our road map and we have traveled this way before
But as we start our engines, we stay blind forever
More destined to a parking lot where ignorance locks the doors.

The Real World

The ugly head of life peers over the edge of reality
and thinks of danger.

Friendship hides in an open field and
awaits certain doom.

Birds circle high and dream of eating
the carcass of humanity and
with every bite, the world sheds a tear
as warmth and kindness becomes a prisoner
until mankind can see the light.

The Winds of Hatred

The hot winds of contempt
blow across the dusty field
sending despair throughout the land.
Coyotes peer from the bushes
with the saliva of hatred dripping from their mouths,
and the poisonous bite of the rattler lures my interest.

Let not the sweet smell of goodwill destroy
this horrid day with the false smile of happiness,
because if done, I'll grab a gun and die a hateful way.

I Will Sleep No More

Yesterday I awoke from a dream
and had a dream, only this dream
was the reality hidden in the fantasy
of life. After all this morning was
my first true appraisal of the thing
called relationship. I spent the better
part of my morning trying to
salvage pennies on the dollar of the
equity invested in my pride,
now standing on the cliff of failure
are the memories of the best days
of my life which no more than
eight hours ago had laid the tracks of
destiny only to awaken too weak and
frail to drive in the final spike.
And now the sun which had always
guided my life is now the lantern
of the fool who will sleep no more.

CHAPTER TWO

A Day of Forest Rain

She looks out of her log cabin everyday
and only thinks of walking through the forest,
which calls for her while she sleeps.

Soon mother nature whispers her an invitation
on the hoot of me, the old owl, who has watched
the forest grow from its conception.

Beads of water tap a tune on her doorstep like
"Fred Astaire" entertaining with a big band,
and with that, her will to resist eroded like the beaver
dam which flows downstream.

Puddles of water leave her no choice but to hopscotch
through the meadow that leads to the mouth of her new home.

The cold damp feel of the forest somehow brought a smile to
her face as I stared from my perch. Words passed quickly and
all of the forest creatures deferred their chores and made ready
for their guest.

The tress that used to look foreign in the past
became commonplace, and as she could see the smoke billowing out
of the fortress she used to call her home, she could see through the
eyes peering at her from the dark, that her world would never
be the same.

A large deer could see her concern and offered her a log to rest her feet,
and when she cleared the tears, which she thought were raindrops, from her eyes,
her new friends walked her home to say good-bye to her past and guide her
to her
seat next to mother nature.

Desert Rose

The sun rises on the horizon and the glare
Which rolls off the back of the desert tortoise
Sets the stage for the garden of the sun.
Flowers bloom from where there is no life
As spring calls for your love to nourish another day.

Soft wind gently kisses your cheek
And whispers my love for you.
Dust storms move like ballroom dances
As coyotes howl a tune of passion.

Suddenly the sound of thunder makes the horizon
rumble

A Day In The Forest

Snowflakes float down to earth
laying the print work for the forest floor.
Hoof prints mark out trails
that vanish as soon as they appear.
The giant redwoods stand in defiance
to the skyscrapers on the horizon.

A community meeting is held by the wolves
about the forthcoming hunt.
Moving in the background, are grazing deer
awaiting their time to join the food chain.
A bald eagle flies overhead trying to disassociate
itself from the ground dwellers.
The flying squirrels boast they have
the best of both worlds
And with that the eagle forces them to choose
the trees or death.
They choose life, with the gratification of a short
stay with the Gods.

Nightfall comes and the changing
of the guards is complete
The blue-collar workers prepare
for their reign of the forest.
Glowing eyes now mark the trail
and rattlesnakes act as centuries
and escort me out of their home.

Kim's Treetops

Love fills the air with the smell of the blossoms illuminating
the sky with their taste of passion.
And today, like every other, Kim's walk through the
orchard never turns out the same way, as new adventures
mount their horses in pursuit of destiny.

Deep in the back, her private tree house shows how her freedom
serves as Mother Nature's last refuge and why
the walls of her home are covered with the finest
leaves and bark from her trees.

Soon Kim finds the need for music and the birds
bathing in her pond sing a tune that kisses her
eyelids shut as the day's work goes undone,
even though the sun's rays try and pull her closer
to the door only to have the night pull back the
covers and whisper "goodnight".

Nature's Portrait

The brisk sea breeze rushes over the waves
Pushing the tide into the shore and as I look outward,
The ocean waves match the graceful flow of your hair

Seagulls break from their formation
And with the backdrop of the clouds,
Nature has made a portrait of the beauty
That can only be seen by the soul.

I start to run sand through my fingers
And as each grain touches the earth,
My mind remembers every time we've met,
And as the last grain falls to the ground,
My heart roars with the pain of the times you've left.

So forever, when I sit on the beach
And watch the sand fall downward through my fingers,
The sky will always be your smile
And each grain your touch.

World With A View

Walking through the meadows
leaves crackling with my every step
and my heart soars to the top of the
snow capped mountains in the view ahead.

Society is acted out by the diligent beavers at play
and I have only my heartbeat to keep me aware
That the trees and I are witness to
a picture of life that has come and may leave
But will always live in the mind of mother nature.

Summer's Dance With Winter

Sunlight from the hillside to the seas
shows the change of summer's eve
As the strong hand of winter guides
warmth to it's resting place in the
bosom of winter
Today has made yesterday into tomorrow
connecting the seasons which holds
the fabric of nature together in its
constant dance with change

Butterfly

Butterflies fill the air with the
colors of the rainbow, and as you
walk they follow you like waves
in a pond. The sunlight graciously
shines on your seductive curves as
you move into the sunset.

Swans carry your smile into the
hearts of the world. And with one
look in your eyes, love and kindness
consumes the worries of mankind.

Tsunami

Silence pounds a deaf drum through the world
I swim for my life
As the noises made by my quiet paddle talks me into staying alive for at least
one day
Clouds look down on me from the stadium set in heaven
And applaud my efforts even if they only prolong the game that has no end
Now facing my final minutes my pain subsides to at least intolerable
Making tomorrow something of the past
And with the power of Neptune himself do I invite
A 40 foot tidal wave to crash down and join me at last!!!

CHAPTER THREE

Soldier Story

Blood stains map out the road to conquest
Lizard meat is served with the graces of a five-star restaurant
and a dusty rock serves as your mother's best china.
Machine gun fire makes for perfect dinner music.
Every bite keeps you closer to life because in your heart,
death is the only guarantee.

Nightfall brings confusion and allies become enemies
Years of hard training are shadowed by childhood fears
And with the dying words of the sergeant, you take command.

Daybreak turns your stomach, three new graves are filled.
Your eulogy is short and sweet. ("You die for nothing
and we join you soon").

Morale is high because three of our guys have left hell.
The following day finds the white of hospital sheets over you.
It's clear, my men have all made it to a better place.
I'm the only survivor left with the job of brining flowers
on Veteran's Day. The only time I really live.

Red T-Shirts, White Sheets

One long face makes the look of an adventure
Hours of naval gunfire rings the door bell of hell
With our gear accounted for down to the last round
in your heart fear still goes unaccounted for in formation
The ocean a crystal blue awaits the red that follows the corps amphibious
house call
Bushes move up and down, side to side which keeps my aim at full attention
Charlie, still asleep in underground tunnels, prepares to join their ancestors
as we speak
The water starts to attack our soul when the first wave fights to get past the
reef which holds up victory
Marines finally come ashore using their bodies as a bridge when heavy gunfire
changes the uniform of the day from green utilities to the red suits of death
Funerals last as long as it takes to reload our 50 cal
The first sergeant yells "keep your head down" and moves out, hunger looks
for a quiet place to dine
So the thought of killing the enemy for breakfast gives blood the taste of
orange juice
And just like cutting a piece of toast in half I rip off Charlie's head
Now with the taste of blood gently running down my face the hole in my
arm seems almost worthwhile
Our first wave is complete and all we have to show for it is red t-shirts and
white sheets

Tribute To the Corps

Thunder rolls through my heart as the call to
protect my country overrides my need for personal safety.
Thousands of eyes share the same view
as the battlefield grows near and the chains around their
necks pull taut as the soul of destiny peeks out
from the growls of defense, USMC clearly shown in their pride, as the world's fears
come true as 'Devil Dogs' shock troops enter the conflict.

The beachhead, now the marketplace for confusion,
only has the steady trail of blood to show the direction
of democracy as the bodies of marines and enemies alike
propels the Corps into the final conflict.

The sound of helos and the smell of charred flesh awaken
me as my comrades go through rubble and pull the last of the
surviving good men on their way back to sea, where amphibious
assault awaits his children back from another day at play
that ends with a stare off of the fantail of destiny.

Marine Corps Sniper

The fog of war rolls in and out of the swamp the same way
his mother would pull the covers over his shoulders
when he would fall asleep on the couch.
But sleep is the last thought going through the mind of the
commissioner of death.

Today brings good luck. A parade starts in the distance and
as they turn the first corner, the eyes on the lead float move
and clearly show the head of a python. Down periscope
is sounded and death submerges, leaving his adversary to
whisper Run Silent, Run Deep.

Hours climb on the backs of days in search of weeks
with only the bite of leeches to move the second hand.
Time stops, then in slow-mo his eyes turn into cross arrows
as water drips from the barrel, one shot, one kill.
The sound of the body hitting the ground is matched by the
thunder that turns into a silhouette hanging on a rope
behind a helo rushing back to their home, which bares the
seal, EAGLE, GLOBE, and ANCHOR.

Marine Integrity

Decisions are made without any doubt
In addition, the views of the whole make up the catalyst of his response to
the truth
And with his futuristic goals becoming a part of today
Everything he touches takes on the proud glow of glory that walks hand in
hand alongside every marine
Which has an eagle, globe and anchor branded on his soul
It has been said that the marine was conceived from the mother of truth and
the father of dedication and raised to be the example of mankind.

Dedication

Gale force winds press down on the stern jaw of the Corps
As conquest reaches out to give the Corps a helping hand onto the ledge of victory
Years of hard work melt into the iron used to cast the armor which only fits the true
When dedication calls on the very fiber of its existence which turns storm clouds and rough seas into the cool ocean spray at the end of a difficult day that brings freedom to a world which finds comfort in the strong hand of the Corps.

Intestinal Fortitude

The trail to victory grows dark as the
Longest day turns into the longest night.
Dedication to duty propels our every step as
The word Marines is spoken like a command
From God erase fear, loneliness and the very
Thought of hesitation from the mind of
The world's finest fighting force U.S. Marines
So when word of failure knocks at our
Door our belief, strength and determination
Welcomes the challenge of a new world.

Road to Destiny

Quiet sat next to silence on the ride to destiny
As the lights in the distance turn into our future
The bus we were on had to be fueled by our anticipation because when
We listened for the engine our heart beats matched the sound of the pistons
striking the deck
Slowly the eyes of fear peered out of the head of commitment
As the driver turned into a sergeant of the U. S. Marines
And said this is a time for sleep tomorrow we'll have none
We dreamed of forgiveness as the bus starts to rumble like a thousand strikes
of lightning
The driver yells silence as a graduating platoon marches by our bus
And inside we all wonder if we have what it takes to be the few, the proud,
a U.S. Marine

Forward Observer

The morning still hours away as the stealth messenger stares out of his shelter half
The rain still making its way to the front line fills in the footprints of those
who walk alone
So as he quietly disappears into the night his mission closes out the rest of
the war
Trees become safe havens when danger passes without a word
As a blueprint of the scene is carefully documented and put with the other
pieces of the puzzle
Each part of his mind works for the good of all as loneliness tightens its grip
on his discipline
Bad luck comes on the wings of large birds which give away his position
Gunfire sends rounds echoing all around his body and with the holes in his
chest slowly making a river out of his blood does the years of training pay off
as he radios in his last transmission
That gives the corps not only a look ahead but a look at the future.

Patrol

Another night starts his prey on the fear
of the Corps as each trail takes on
a life of their own and each step is covered by
the next only to make a simple deviation
as costly as not beating a train at its crossing
Eyes stare with the beams of the
hated only to ask forgiveness after you
serve another night of being the head light
Of death. A call to order stops
the heart of doom as the jungle
Calls for the next to play
His hand in the poker game of life.

Small Price To Pay

Eyes link together the madness as raindrops secure
hope for another night. The quiet made by our
fears is only matched by the empty bottle of Johnny
Walker Black that we now use as a card table. Footstep
come closer and turn into a marine dead tired and
ready to be replaced on the frontline, so with my
last swig of water running down my face does the
cost of freedom mean so much. Sometime we
try and think of this war as a field trip with
the Boy Scouts until mail call doesn't bring bags
of cookies, just more boxes of body bags and the
Vietcong gives classes on tying knots only to
fully instill fear as class ends when the rope
is connected to a marine's neck hanging from
his observation post and we wonder if the
change in his pocket is really such a small
price to pay.

CHAPTER FOUR

Survival At Sea

Daybreak brings another low
The seas have calmed but still I have no companion
Driftwood passes by and I see them as
battleships maneuvering for positioning in
their brief passing.

Soon the sound of the guns fades away.
Sunrise turns the ocean into a glass table
and seahawks dive for their morning meal.

Hunger far exceeds my desire for friendship
and sharks come by and remind me that life could
turn for the worse.

My dreams still show grief for the others
who died on the sinking ship.
But does God think of me as the lone survivor
at sea?

My last thoughts before I join my comrades.

South Sea Dream

Small waves roll into the distance,
sea hawks lay in wait for schools of fish
and you float on your raft trying to
make the clouds into portraits of your desire.

Friendly seas make way for your arrival
to the shore of an island as warm as your smile
and as caring as your heart.

You dream of your south sea paradise
and find out you make paradise
of every place you go.

Juke Box Diner

The crackling of bacon keeps everybody's feet tapping
in between the last record played in the juke box as Ed Jones
fumbles his last quarter in the slot.

And there is the look on the face of a stranger, who can't believe
there are no menus, because Lizzy, the owner, tells everyone what
she's cookin today.

High noon is sounded by a carefully aimed shot in the spit patoon
over yonder, and the Sunday paper seems hard to read when it shows
up on Monday. but that's life at the Juke Box Diner, where you're always
one quarter away from silence and one meal from starvation.

Wind Storm

The sky let out a howl that I will remember forever.
The sound echoed through my soul and each
vibration shook loose another piece of the puzzle
of love, because the last time the heavens opened up they
took my heart with it.

My eye which I use as a window as I look for her to come home,
gathers residue when hope tempts me with the shadow of a
woman that can't exist. Time, which has little value,
whispers for me to wait a few minutes longer because without
my hope, this world will end and purgatory will rule forever.

The sun cracks through the clouds and I see your
smile in every drop of sunlight. Soon the moisture
that used to be my tears dries up and leaves me destined
to wait for another storm, another dream, another day
without a life that lives and dies by the coming of your storm.

To Shade A Friend

Once my world grew straight up to the stars
and my hope of the future had a firm place with life.
But as the clouds moved to the forefront, my view
of happiness formed the tears that made the rain
which washed away and grew my destiny
until friendship walked up to me on the shadow of a
tree that at one time was my adversary.

And now I find out it was the only friend I had that
stood next to me through the storms of strife and pain.
Together our future is not clear but as long as our
shadow covers each other, we have hope.

Sunset To Sunset

It was like the light of a thousand years, but yet every
strand of light felt like the first time my eyelids dropped into the
ocean of love, that brought hope for a new tomorrow.

And even though her beauty was too bright to see,
the care in my heart gave my vision the strength
to see deep into her soul. One night, out of the fear of losing her,
I reached up and made my arms into the sky
and tied together a sunset to a sunrise,
so that I would never have to live another night
without the warmth, love and tender kisses that her
sunset brings to the night.

And when the morning came, I was met by today and love told me of tomorrow.

Come Back To Me

My head firmly against your chest puts my mind at ease,
so when your kiss on my forehead says good-bye, jealousy
fills my heart.

Today, which I know is 24 hours, seems too short as I find
myself selling parts of my soul for a memory of our time together.

Shadows of clouds passing by mock my love for you as they
make formations that look like our last kiss and my stare
into the heavens says come back to me.

Sit Down By A Stream

Unknown counties border a stream marked
by its hope for tomorrow. Once as a child,
my mother made mention of a beautiful girl
whose love for a man she had never met,
stopped the stream for the one that would
cross to join her love.

So everyday I walk up to the shore and look at my
reflection and dream of your smile and even though
I only remember how she made me feel, our first glance
will be as familiar as the sun rising from the east.

Years pass before your love came home and just as I was about
to lose belief in the world, for one second the water
stood still and my reflection walked across and for the first
time our lips touched in the shadow of the stream
when forever rose up from commitment and
joined together our passion, making our counties one.

Lone Wolf

Dry, lonely, and still carves a quiet trail through the crowd
which turns its back on me every time friendship
pours the last beer in a dirty glass with a hole in it.

Just in time to toast goodwill and a fond good-bye, weeks stand
up like months when years shake hands with death.

Abandoned

Darkness falls and my heartbeat drowns the sound of the jungle.
My herd has moved across the river now
leaving me to take on the attack of the oncoming wolves.
The damage to my leg has given me no chance to escape
so fear stands in amazement as I call for my enemies.
Soon I'm surrounded by their eyes,
all laughing at my untimely demise.
Voices come out of my soul and say
"May God be with you".
My enemies, hundred strong, soon
feel their weakness as I reveal the
twenty pounds of explosives underneath
my flak jacket. I yell "Good luck!" as
once abandoned in life, my comrades and I
are joined forever.

The Bus Ride

Harsh looks plant the seed of hatred
in the fertile soil of my mind.
The lack of direction makes the ride
long with anticipation.

I struggle for my change and find my
fare has been paid by the unsteadiness of my mind.
Heavy bindings hold me upright as my freedom to
fall is destroyed, and the driver taunts us with his control.
I dream of choking him with a mental rope, but as
it tightens, his lack of reality sets him free.
The doors of the bus open and it's all clear to me now
We have arrived at the state mental facility.